Little Jamie In Paradise

by Dom Léon Robert, O.S.B.

monk of Solesmes

(1896 - 1969)

Translated by

Dom Lawrence Brown, O.S.B.

monk of Clear Creek Abbey

Abbey Editions

Abbey Editions

Our Lady of Clear Creek Abbey

Hulbert, Oklahoma

www.clearcreekmonks.org

© 2024 Our Lady of Clear Creek Abbey

ISBN: 979-8-9887311-4-6

"Consider the lilies of the field, how they grow."

- St. Matt. 6:28

Little Jamie had been ill now for several days. No longer did Mama get him up and dress him every morning; and at night it was a long time before sleep came to his eyes. He was all covered with sweat and shook with fever—oh, such strange sensations—to the point that he did not even know if he was suffering. Days and long nights were spent staring at the patterns of light and shadow playing in the folds of the bed-curtains or listening to the mysterious hum that filled his ears—the thumping of his heart which seemed to run and jump in his chest. He could not quite come to understand what was happening. Why did they leave him like this? Why did Mama not lift from off his chest this terrible weight which was suffocating him? And why did she seem to cry all the while? He could see it was because of him. Just the same, he had done nothing wrong, no one had scolded him for anything; just for once he was trying to be so very very good!

The doctor had come several times already. His big gray and wrinkled head bent down over him, his ear against Jamie's back listening; Jamie was not afraid and politely let him listen. That evening the doctor had come again but had not stayed very long. A few words spoken softly and he was gone. Then Mama leaned down over him and kissed him tenderly.

—"You know you are soon going to see little Jesus."

These were words of joy bringing good news...

—"You will tell little Jesus to come and get me right away; you won't forget, will you?"

Jamie answered nothing; his big eyes bright with fever, were fixed upon the moist eyes of his mother.

—"You will tell little Jesus, won't you?"

—"Yes, Mama."

—"And then, you will be good up there, won't you?"

Poor Mama, she did not really know what she was saying. This was her usual recommendation when she would send him out to play with cousins or friends. She was just looking out for his reputation; she did not want anyone in the world to say that her little boy had been poorly raised; Jamie murmured again, "Yes, Mama."

Papa came to speak to him, but Jamie could not understand all it was he said. He let himself be held for a long time, a long long time, when finally things ended up in a blur.

Night came. The little lamp placed by the curtains of his bed offered a hesitant glimmer which he had contemplated many times during the endless nights. The roar of his heart, the fever at its height, the light which seemed to grow fainter, his eyes wide open, he had the impression he was being swallowed by the shadows... Finally, little Jamie slipped away into a great sleep...

❀ ❀ ❀ ❀ ❀

...the sound of children's voices woke him.

Totally astonished, Jamie opened his eyes. Behold, it was daylight. It seemed that he had slept ages and that this sleep had completely changed him. No more of feeling tired, no more fever, but rather such a sense of well-being which he had never felt, so alert and glad to be alive. No doubt Mama had opened the windows because through the curtains of his little bed an immense bright light was to be seen; yet it was a very soft, a very pure light, and one which filled his eyes with marvelous things. But both this healing and this light were as nothing; little children can hardly pay attention to several things at once, and what was drawing Jamie's attention was the startling fact that the room where he had been sick was now entirely filled with little children. What a surprise! They were on all sides of his bed, all of them speaking at the same time and wanting to see. It is something very important for a boy to find himself all at once in the presence of many young children he does not know. A bit anxious, Jamie waited to see what was going to happen.

Then a well-known voice said, "Come children; see your new little brother."

At the same time the curtains parted and Jamie saw. Sure enough, he was surrounded by a crowd of little children, the oldest of which was surely not over seven. Only you could not say the room was filled as there was no longer any room, nor was he any longer in his parents' house. No more walls, no ceiling, but instead, a blue sky everywhere. And around his bed were hundreds of eyes, wide-open eyes all fixed on him. He too looked at them in amazement. Then up he sat and, half out of the covers, remained dumb with wonder and secretly intimidated.

The little children, on the other hand, were neither still nor intimidated; quite the contrary, it was a sea of heads ruffled by the wind... All around the bedstead at least thirty little hands were pulling desperately at the rail—children hoping to get a better look and acting as if they wanted to take the bed by storm. It was a confused mass of eyes of all colors and hair of all sorts: curly or straight, blond or brown, long or short. There were small little mouths which laughed or sang or told Jamie how very nice he was and how everyone liked him a lot; others asked when they could play together and many other good things. And there was a little boy carrying a huge palm branch that put a pleasant blotch of green (and prickly points!) in the midst of all these round rosy faces.

At the far edge of the group surrounding his bed, Jamie caught sight of a bigger girl and a bigger boy who seemed to be about twelve or thirteen years old. Both were watching over the group of children, and would lift up the smaller ones, who were unable to see Jamie, so they could have the joy of greeting him, if only at a distance. Those who had not yet gotten a good look were jumping with impatience, annoying their guardians:—"Now me!"—"Agnes, it's my turn!"—"Tarcisius, let me see again!" And Tarcisius and Agnes would laugh and do their best to satisfy all their demands.

Suddenly one of the children yelling louder than the others cried, "Mother, Mother, what is the name of our new little brother?"

And the same voice that had once already spoken replied, "Jamie."

"Oh, like me," yelled a good half dozen little boys all at the same time. And one of them added: "If you are called Jamie, then you'll have to come and play with us!"

Immediately the silence and calm which, more or less, had lasted during this exchange of words, was violently interrupted. Everyone started moving and talking and showing an equal eagerness to go play right away with their new little brother.

It was touching to see their enthusiasm. And he was the cause of it, just think of that! Jamie could hardly believe it. There was no possible doubt about it; it was really, because of him, just him, that all these children were so happy. It was Jamie that they had been waiting for with such impatience. It was to see him that they were all pressed around his bed and all were waiting to have him for company in their games. Perhaps their mothers had asked them to be nice to Jamie and share their toys, or else be scolded. But no, it was spontaneous joy, like on a long-awaited feast day. It was his turn now to smile at all these children who were there smiling at him. How they must be fun to play with! They were certainly well behaved, even though there were so many; and there was not a single one that did not look perfectly happy. It was really astonishing; normally in a group of children it is hard to keep one or another from pouting or playing pranks or just crying. But Jamie had the impression that in the place where he was, there could never be found anything bothersome or sad, never a scene with tears. Older persons there must have known nothing of what it is like to scold children. In any case, noise was certainly not forbidden.

Again the same kind and joyful voice was heard: "Yes, you may all play with Jamie, but each in turn as usual. Oh, but first of all let me take him into my arms."

Who was speaking in that manner? Jamie looked but could not see, because the curtain to one side of his bed had not been opened. He was trying to lean out a bit to get a look, when finally the curtain was drawn back revealing the woman who had spoken, who now bent down over his bed to lovingly contemplate her new little boy.

❀ ❀ ❀ ❀ ❀

Oh, how Jamie was dazzled! The wonder of it all! It was so far beyond him!

All the nice little boys who were, without a doubt, better and nicer than those he had ever known before, were all—he had seen it right from the beginning—not so different from himself; but Her! So much beauty and gentleness, such splendor, and so close and attentive to someone so small! How can you describe her? She was clothed in a blue gown, her long hair fell over her shoulders, and by way of ornament she wore around her head a fine band of gold. It was not an ordinary blue, nor a gold like any other; they seemed somehow soft and living like light itself. The blue and gold of the sky's light seemed curiously related to the blue and gold Jamie beheld. And there were her eyes, too, very large, and her small mouth whose smile, made of joy and kindness, seemed to poke fun at him. She appeared to be amused by the unlimited wonder she was causing Jamie.

—"Don't you recognize your own Mother?"

Oh such sweet words! Suddenly, overflowing with gladness, Jamie started to laugh: how could he fail to recognize his own Mother?! Nevertheless, it was the first time he had ever seen her; only, she looked at him with such jealous tenderness that it was obvious, irresistibly obvious, that Jamie had never belonged so much to anyone else. So it was out of so much joy that Jamie laughed. It was so good to see that Our Lady, too, was perfectly happy, as if her new little boy had greeted her better than she had expected.

It was as in past mornings when he awoke to see the attentive and loving face of she who, the night before, had put him to bed and kissed him just before sleep closed his eyes. But now these sensations were a hundred, a thousand times stronger. This really was an extraordinary awakening; moreover what charmed him most was the joyful confidence, the total abandon which he felt in the presence of his Mother. From now on nothing could be wanting; and soon he would be where every child always wants to be: in the arms of his Mother, arms like a fortress or a tower of ivory, where one is safe from all dangers; arms that are a throne, a hiding place, a house of gold. Oh, he so wanted to be lifted into the arms of Our Lady, hidden in the blue shadows of her veil, pressed against the freshness of her cheek and covered with the kisses of her small, fine mouth.

Our Lady sensed with growing joy the longing of her little Jamie's heart. She enjoyed making it last until she herself could wait no longer, and had to have her treasure, snatching him from off his bed, pressing him against her heart and covering him with kisses. She seemed to feel a real maternal pride in having such a sweet little boy. Normally little boys do not understand that they are the glory of their mothers; it was even harder here. Yet just the same, Jamie could not help but see the happiness he was causing Our Lady. She already had many other children, but they too were loved in this same unique love. To love them like this they must have cost her very much.

For the moment it was as if Jamie alone were her happiness. She just went on contemplating him and whispering to him between kisses. She said things like, "My little Jamie, my handsome little boy." He clung to his Mother, cuddling against her shoulder, trying to lose himself in her arms or in the folds of her veil or in the velvety curls of her fine, long hair. He had the impression he was lost in living joy. The mysterious perfumes of his Mother made him dizzy with their sweetness; it was as if he were in a well-closed garden whose flowers had given Our Lady their delicate odors: the lily of the field, the rose, balm and perhaps the resinous incense that comes from the cedar and cypress trees of the East, Our Lady was fragrant with the divine fragrances of the Child Jesus.

These first moments of heavenly joy were to give place to others still more heavenly. Our Lady placed Jamie in her left arm and said:

—"Now we shall go see the Lord Jesus. Would you like that?"

Would Jamie like that?! He was at the peak of his joy; but Our Lady held him so tight that he could not even answer yes. Then the Blessed Virgin turned towards the other children there, who were displaying great joy for so much that reminded them of their own birth into Heaven. "Children," she said, "follow

Tarcisius who is going to lead you back to your garden. You, Agnes, come with us; when my Lord Jesus has blessed Jamie, you will bring him back to rejoin the others." So Our Lady, carrying Jamie and followed by Agnes, set out for the throne of God.

≈ ≈ ≈ ≈ ≈

Jamie's heart felt something like an emotion, for here he was in the arms of Our Lady, in the same place where the Child Jesus sat. What was little Jesus going to say to that? The eyes of little Jamie eagerly questioned those of Our Lady, seeking to guess how things were going to turn out. But the Blessed Virgin, enjoying the perplexity of her little boy, made no reply. She hurried up the three steps of the throne; there, Jamie had his explanation.

First of all, little Jesus was not at all little. He was a man, tall and handsome; obviously the small hands of Our Lady could no longer carry Him. Jamie saw that it was better that way, and, in fact, it could not be otherwise. Or rather, this fact imposed itself upon him without his being entirely conscious of it, for right away something else captured his attention. Our Lord was seated on a throne decked with many sorts of cushions, and He was all dressed in white. His hair, parted in the middle of his brow, fell down on each side of His head and formed at His shoulder a handsome curl. He was all strength and kindness. He took Jamie on His knees and Jamie, who had already seen marvel upon marvel, found himself in the presence of something that surpassed them all: the eyes of the Lord Jesus.

All that he saw there was inexpressible, though the impression it made on him was not entirely new. When first he had awakened to the light of Heaven, his eyes had been mysteriously prepared to see what now he saw. Jamie beheld so many things in the eyes of the Lord.

For the moment Jamie did not seek to distinguish or count the details of the riches which were offered there, because they gave themselves so freely, with nothing for you to do but receive them all. Between Jesus and himself, from eye to eye, there was a give-and-take, a flow of life, tenderness and intense joy sinking to the innermost region of the soul. All that had existed inside of him was as if renewed. It was like a river where he could drink and swim, submerged in unspeakable delight.

Here, then, was a revelation of God, soft, quiet, calm, filling the heart with so much joy and light which contain them, the heart must have widened itself infinitely. There were no words exchanged, and yet what things had been said.

Happily he had all eternity before him. Jamie felt he would never have too much leisure to recall one of the graces that were given him at that instant, and about which he had but a confused idea. He understood only that his Creator had now finished the work of his creation and that he, so weak and tiny, was the object of all the loving attention of HE WHO IS, the infinitely almighty. Without a sound the Lord pronounced a name upon him, his real name, a new name, yet so very old. For God, from all eternity and before all centuries, had loved and desired little Jamie. When, by the sole act of His will, the universe was created in the one magnificent Word which made all things exist and grow before Him in His sight, this same unique name was included, this name which contained all that time reserved for Jamie in the way of graces of being, of life and of beatitude. Now the time had come for this name to be revealed to him, and him alone, or more exactly, to be definitively imprinted in him by his Creator, thereby ending and crowning Jamie's creation. The name was both mysterious and powerful; no other mouth could ever say it and no one else ever know it but God and Jamie; a name that God repeats endlessly in the hearts of His Saints as if to call them closer and closer to Himself.

Jamie went on adoring. He saw God. He saw his Creator, and in Him saw all things as a work of His almighty love. And Jamie gave himself, surrendered himself, lost himself completely in God.

How long did this silent conversation last? How can you speak of time in the midst of eternity? The Lord spoke a few words to make an end: "This is my creature Jamie, whom I have loved; he is as I conceived him."

These human words caused Jamie to come out of a sort of ecstasy into which he had fallen; the eyes of the Lord seemed to allow him to regain consciousness of other things. Jamie was a bit astonished to find himself standing on the knees of the Lord, exactly as he used to do on his Papa's knees. Curious mixture of things wonderful and familiar habits. The Lord then drew a small cross on his forehead as if to retrace the one which was drawn there at his baptism; He embraced him and gave him back to Our Lady who was seated at His side.

It was then that Jamie remembered the promise he had made to his other mother. Now how to go about it? How do you speak about your first mother to your real Mother?

Happily his prayer was understood by Our Lady without it having to be said. It was becoming obvious there was nothing hidden from her. She leaned slightly towards the Lord and murmured: "Jamie's mother would be happy here."

The Lord smiled, and after looking with great kindness at Jamie, simply said, "And if I preferred she remain a little longer on Earth?"

Oh, in that case! If that is what God wanted, then Jamie wanted it too, of course, and so did his mother. And as if He wished to explain His reason for so wanting, the Lord Jesus added: "Isn't it necessary that I suffer still longer in her person?"

Jamie then received a revelation of Our Lord's esteem for the parents which he had been given. He was only a little boy loved and cherished, but they were useful to God; God still had need of them on Earth. Jamie was filled with admiration and thankfulness.

Suddenly the Lord asked, "And Agnes, why doesn't she come?" In a bound Agnes was around Jesus' neck. This swift, familiar gesture of His little bride seemed to please the Lord.

They remained embraced a long while.

❧ ❧ ❧ ❧ ❧

Now that introductions were over, Agnes said, "Come on," and taking Jamie by the hand they were off.

Jamie was overjoyed. From now on he was part of the society of Saints; he was now forever in Heaven. He had a Father and a Mother he loved and who loved him; and he knew that to please them he had nothing else to do but play in their sight with his little brothers. He could not wait to see something of the gardens where it would be so fun to play. The word "garden" by itself suggested so many things already.

They made their way down the steps of the throne: one, two… seven.

Once off the thick and sumptuous carpet, they crossed a wide space covered with polished marble. Jamie found it fun to walk on, cool but not cold under his bare feet. They came down yet another little step and were on golden sand, fine and soft, which like a circular walkway surrounded the great marble floor in front of the throne. Beyond were the gardens of Paradise. Just a few steps and they were in the garden spreading out nearest before the Lord's throne.

"Here is the Children's Garden," said Agnes, "here is where you will be playing for all eternity."

Sure enough, Jamie saw that the garden was filled with children like those he had seen around his bed when first he had awakened. They formed a countless throng; never had he seen so many children together. They were playing. And what were they playing? Children's games, games which have no names, games grown-ups can no longer understand why they are amusing. There were lots of toys scattered about—in the grass, on the paths—balls, crowns, lamps, a big woolly sheep which let itself be climbed upon, and marvelous things which can only be found in Paradise.

Jamie was wonderfully surprised to see lots of little children playing around a huge fountain spouting water in the middle. That he was in a world other than the one he had recently left became obvious to him. On Earth it was expressly forbidden to go too close, here such laws were completely unknown, implying a rule of unimaginable liberty!

They stopped to look.

Agnes saw right away that Jamie was fascinated by the fountain, "Listen," she said, "do you want to go play right away or would you prefer to visit the other gardens beforehand?"

At the same time Agnes spun Jamie around to let him view the whole of Paradise spread out like a vast wonderful countryside.

It was a whole new world, and all of its parts were visible at once, all of radiant beauty. For a long moment Jamie just stood there gaping in admiration, as if stunned by this new flood of marvels. It was only after having gotten used to it little by little that he began to make out some of the details.

The center was occupied by the throne of God wherein was seated the Lord, all dressed in white, and to His right Our Lady, clad in blue and gently leaning against His shoulder. The train of their robes spread out in large folds over the checkered black and white squares of a vast rectangular marble floor. Beyond was the path of fine sand.

Surrounding the sandy walk and throne were fourteen gardens, like the one the children were playing in, full of pleasant green grass, wide sandy pathways, beds of flowers, fountains, pools and large shady trees. The cypress and the yew seemed to loom above the others; magnificent trees they were, straight and lofty, certainly more than a thousand years old.

As they advanced farther from the center of Paradise, the gardens rose gradually from terrace to terrace by way of stately, white marble steps, until finally they merged with what were real hills. On the horizon the trees blended together and spread everywhere forming a great forest which encompassed all of Paradise.

What was there beyond that? Probably Limbo; at any rate, once past the crests of the hills one certainly could no longer see the Good Lord.

The entire landscape was bathed in a dazzling but gentle light. What a strange light! In fact, this was perhaps the uncreated light itself, a light Jamie sensed confusedly as being alive; but how could that be? Turning away from the distant horizon, he looked back towards the Lord and discovered at least part of the solution: this light emanated from Him. Clothed in white vestments, Jesus alone was the source of all light in Heaven; all things were visible by virtue of Him. And it seemed as though it were by this light radiating from Him that Jesus reached out, touched and poured into each creature His life, His beauty, His joy. Jamie noticed, too, that if all of Heaven's light came from the Lord, the color blue, on the other hand, had no other origin than the reflections coming from the Blessed Virgin's veil. Finally, this light gave to the immensity of Paradise, and to the multitude of the Blessed that live there, its profound unity.

Yes, the Blessed were there in countless numbers, though even the word "countless" is feeble to designate all those whom the gardens seemed hardly to be able to contain. It was as if all of humanity living on Earth at this moment, and more, were assembled at the same time, in the same place. Even so, everything was in perfect order, and each of the Saints had a very good place to occupy; which kept no one from going wherever he pleased to visit someone, or go to the Lord to receive some blessing. Thus a calm animation reigned in the gardens, while around the throne of God was a constant coming-and-going. Some of the Saints seemed to be ever seated on the steps of the throne; the one there at the feet of the Lord could scarcely be anyone else but Saint Mary Magdalen. Jamie knew that the two noble handmaids near Our Lady were Queen Esther and Saint Elizabeth of Hungary.

The fourteen gardens were laid out in such a way as to have six to the right and six to the left of the throne, and two in front. The six gardens at the right were home for six categories of men Saints, beginning with the martyrs. In the six to the left lived the glorious daughters of Eve, beginning also with their martyrs. Across from each of these twelve gardens was a throne of honor seating one of the twelve Apostles. Each Apostle presided over the hymn of praise and adoration which rose from the garden in front of him. This was probably the manner in which they ruled over the twelve tribes of the new Israel.

The two gardens just in front of the throne of God were reserved, one for the children, the other for the virgins. No one presided over their hymns as there is no intermediary between them and the Lord. To the right, on the side of the men martyrs, were the children; the virgins on the left.

Virgins and children, both were clothed in white. It was not so for the other Saints. In their gardens what a sumptuous show of costumes of the most magnificent and vivid colors, reminding Jamie of certain stained-glass windows he had seen in churches, but much more beautiful. The Saints in these gardens all wore sparkling jewels, crowns or diadems, bracelets and broaches, scepters and still other precious ornaments. Soldiers and kings bore arms of great worth.

But this glittering array paled before the simple band of fine gold encircling the brow of Our Lady. Really, this alone appeared to be pure gold.

When contemplating the gentle Virgin in her veil of blue, all the rest seemed to grow dull, as if seen through a mist. And when one looked at the Lord, it was simple: all the rest disappeared. He had no ornament whatsoever—nor precious stones, nor crown, nor scepter; He was His own glory, and all others faded before Him. Really, there was only the Lord Jesus.

Little Jamie well saw that without Jesus the gardens of Paradise would be nothing at all. He accounted for their existence, He was their foundation, their light, the joy of life therein; the beauty, happiness, love and praise of everything that lived here in Paradise flowed from Him.

Having understood these things, Jamie felt glad and infinitely grateful.

✶ ✶ ✶ ✶ ✶

This time his mind was made up.

When Agnes asked him if he wanted to go play right away or go over into the gardens, he answered promptly:

—"I want to go over into the gardens."

And Agnes: "Let's start here then, among the virgins; they will be very glad to meet you."

It is a well known fact in Heaven that the virgins have a weak spot for little children.

Agnes took Jamie and, hand in hand, they went down the sandy path towards the Virgins' Garden. As they were walking along, she pointed out flowers and trees and other things they saw. Having crossed a bordering row of lilies that formed the limits of this garden, they stopped again.

"Listen, Jamie," said Agnes, "I do think it would be good if you tidied up a bit before being introduced to everyone. Stand up straight in front of me and don't move, while I re-do the knot of your cord and the folds of your robe."

Jamie was dressed, like the other children, in a small white robe that came down to his knees and short sleeves. His arms, legs and feet were bare; his robe was held at the waist by a small cord tied in front. His cut of hair was the same as on Earth.

Agnes was half kneeling in front of him and doing her best to arrange her little brother's clothes. "Really! No one would have any trouble seeing you come from Earth! You have no taste down there whatsoever!"

Meanwhile a long lock of her hair slipped down over her shoulder and fell between her hands just so as to bother her. With a gracious movement that only young girls of twelve know how to make, she threw back the unruly tress only to see it slip back almost immediately. A little miffed, she briskly flicked it back again, looking as if she were about to get angry at the insolent lock of hair. Deep down though, she was proud of her hair, and for good reason: long ago it had been of great help to her, and in fact, in all of Paradise there was hardly anyone but Mary Magdalen who had hair more beautiful than hers—except Our Lady, of course.

Jamie noticed a fine gold chain around Agnes' neck as she was fussing over him. A small cross of red coral, that he found to be very pretty, hung from it. Pointing to it with his finger he said all amazed, "A little cross!"

—"Ah! You like my cross, do you? It is pretty, you know! Our Lady said, 'Here is our little Agnes; what will she receive as a reward?' And I saw beside the Lord a big basket full of crowns, diamonds, necklaces and other jewels. The Lord Jesus saw that they were of no interest to me, so He fumbled around in the bottom of the basket until He drew out this small cross of red coral. You cannot imagine how glad I was when He gave it to me! I alone have a cross like this one; there is not another like it in all of Paradise. I treasure it so, and wouldn't lend to anyone... except, of course, if the Lord Jesus asked me to lend it, or the Blessed Virgin Mary."

Little Jamie was in admiration; Saint Agnes was to all evidence a very important person. He made up his mind to be very good and obedient to her. Besides, his tidying-up was now finished; a couple of light brushes to his hair and all was in perfect order—he could make his entry into this new world.

Jamie, however, was used to being hugged when he had been well behaved during his dressing. He considered that to be a good custom and one worth keeping. So he frowned a little bit, just enough to be seen by Agnes who, knowing all about small children, understood right away. And since she wanted to hug Jamie ten times more than he wanted to be hugged, their mutual wish was soon satisfied.

෨ ෨ ෨ ෨ ෨

The reception in the Virgins' Garden was a real success. All of the Saints there wanted to embrace Jamie and hold him in their arms. They could not hide their admiration: one preferred his big eyes, another his little mouth; many, when it was their turn, found him a bit heavy and said with a wink, "He sure is strong for his age!"

Most of them, by way of finery, had nothing more than their beauty and their white robes. Several of them, however, had like Agnes received a jewel. The three saints Jamie liked the most were Saint Joan of Arc, who wore a crown with three fleurs-de-lis in the middle of her forehead, Saint Catherine of Siena, whose necklace was composed of three strings of pearls, and Saint Gertrude, on whose hand shone a brilliant diamond ring.

All of the virgins were equally kind; and Jamie felt so happy in their garden that when it came time to leave, he said timidly, "I sure would like to stay here."

Agnes started laughing: "Oh, no! Dear little brother, that is not possible. How old are you, anyway?"

There was a moment of silence. Jamie seemed to be thinking very hard. He saw clearly what Agnes was getting at. Back on Earth, because he had barely turned five, he had been subject to all kinds of restrictions: children do not speak at the table, children do not talk in front of grown-ups; children must go to bed long before everyone else... Agnes just wanted him to pronounce his own condemnation.

Which is why Jamie was in no hurry to reply to that question. If only he were seven years old... but maybe in Heaven nobody knew his age! Jamie could not count very well and thought that perhaps he had come to the age of reason... between five and seven, maybe there was no big difference. And besides, he had already been in Heaven such a long time... He boldly decided to try his luck.

"I'm seven," he said, looking Agnes straight in the eyes as if it were the most evident thing in the world—one of those innocent looks characteristic of little children who, down deep, are rather crafty.

This sensational declaration met with an immense burst of laughter ringing from one end of Paradise to the other. Burst of laughter? No, one must not exaggerate; it was more like a big smile. In Heaven everything is done with measure and distinction; but there was irony in it just the same, and Jamie understood it perfectly well.

On Earth what embarrassment it used to be to see himself the butt of laughter—and nowhere to go hide his head. Now, to his great surprise, he was not a bit ashamed. Everyone was poking fun at him, but he was happy nevertheless—he was laughing too; and more than anyone else! Not that he was exactly proud of the small sensation he had made—there was nothing to be proud of—it was just that he had obviously succeeded (through no fault of his own) in drawing and fixing upon himself the attention of all the Saints in Heaven. Had it been someone else, attention of this sort might have produced conceit, but not with Jamie. First, because conceit is impossible in Heaven, and because, despite everything, Jamie had a strong feeling he had not become the center of Paradise, even for a few seconds. No, there was only one center of Paradise and everyone knew it, and saw it, and in no way desired that it should change.

What made Jamie so happy, despite this misadventure, was that all of a sudden he had made a great discovery (which goes to show that great discoveries often have causes as small as they are unforeseen): Paradise had shown its unity. Not the unity of its first principle, the Lord—that he had already seen before—but the unity existing among His members. Jamie had not yet finished his tour of Heaven and already he was seen, known and loved by all the members, without exception, of this immense family of our Heavenly Father. Jamie suddenly felt the charm of the interior life, all aflame with love, which animated this huge family. And he discovered that he was a member, a tiny member, of a great whole animated by one life, and vibrant with a common love and a common joy. Each of the Saints was so close, so intimately united to the lives of the others, that the smallest event happening to one of them became the joy of them all.

So great and so profound was this union that everyone sensed the part he had in the whole, and nowhere could be found an obstacle to the liberty or the personality of any person. Jamie understood this perfectly well. This flow of life was for him as much as it was for the others, and it came to find and fill him wherever he might be, bringing him all the happiness he was able to bear.

In Heaven, then, there was but one heart and one soul. And there was something more, there was the joy of brothers meeting after a long leave of absence, of being brought together forever. That is why everybody surrounded little Jamie's first steps in Paradise with such affection and tenderness; and that is why everybody heard Jamie's big fib—think of it: fibbing right in the middle of Heaven and before the face of God! Something so out of the ordinary was certainly worth laughing about!

"Little monster," teased Agnes, "try as hard as you can, you will never be anything but a little boy; so there!"

All things having grown calm, they again took up their walk.

❀ ❀ ❀ ❀ ❀

Just the same, a problem remained that Jamie could not quite solve by himself. That he was a child, well and good. That his garden was the Children's Garden, well and good, also. But what would happen if he were to like another garden better? And

Agnes? And Tarcisius? Were they in their own gardens? Maybe they had serious reasons for being outside of their gardens. He asked Agnes:

—"Why is it you come with us?"

—"Oh! It's very simple; you see, before, I was in the Virgins' Garden with the other virgins. But often I came to visit the Children's Garden or would look over the row of lilies that borders it; I couldn't understand why you were always left alone. Naturally you didn't know how to play games—how could three-year-old children know such things? Really, I didn't understand. So one day I went to see Our Lady and I asked her to let me take care of you all. She asked the Lord who said yes, so I came I was very glad, to be sure. Then Tarcisius saw me there, and so he came too, because he said I did not know any boy's games. He is very nice, Tarcisius; I do like him so. You'll see for yourself when I send you off to play with him."

—"And what if little children want to go into the other garden?"

—"I see what you're getting at; you want to go back to the Virgins' Garden. Don't worry; you'll have your way; but your own garden will always be the Children's Garden."

—"Why?"

—"Why?! Because you are only five and have not committed any sins."

Agnes' tone of voice made it clear that there was nothing more to be said. Jamie, however, was not yet satisfied; no,

24

because the word "sin" did not say much of anything to him. Jamie continued:

—"Have you committed any sins?"

—"Of course!"

She said this with such an air of superiority that you would almost have thought she was proud of it.

—"And all the Saints who are in the other gardens, have they committed sins too?"

—"Certainly! Only Our Lady and you little children have committed no sins at all."

What great news that was! He had thought that not to have committed any sins was a sign of inferiority, and now he learned that neither had Our Lady ever sinned. Things got more and more mysterious....

—"Sin, what is that?" . . .

—"Oh, something very hard to explain, especially to little children."

—"But since you have committed some..."

—"Yes; but I have forgotten so much since then.... and anyway, I can only remember enough to recall how the Lord washed them all away; and now that they are all gone we don't talk about them anymore, we forget them."

—"All right, but still, what is a sin?"

—"Well, if you must know, sin is when you don't love God. Understand?" Jamie cast a glance at the Lord, "No, I don't"

—"I told you so! Besides, I don't understand either. But you know when you are on Earth and don't see God, you can do some awful things, like the people who made me go to Heaven at the age of twelve—they were certainly very cruel."

—"And so?"

—"So that has not prevented them all from coming here. I have asked them several times why they so enjoyed putting me to death."

—"What did they say?"

—"They always said that they no longer understood why they did it, that they had been wicked, and that if they were in Heaven it was because I had prayed for them. They come quite often to see me and ask me to explain the revelations they receive, because I am charged to instruct them."

Truly, Agnes was an important person. Talking with her became more and more interesting.

—"What else can you tell me?"

—"Well, that is about all there is to it. If we had to answer all the questions little boys ask, eternity itself would be too short a time."

Thereupon they entered the Martyrs' Garden.

Whereas the Virgins' Garden and the Children's Garden were separated by a row of lilies, the other gardens had as boundaries hedges of flowering roses. These gardens varied in size and beauty. The sixth and last garden had fewer flowers than the others, but was still very lovely and pleasant; it was also the biggest. Way in the back, it joined the last garden of Saints, which was likewise immense. These two gardens made up a good third of Paradise.

A good third? Yes, and bit more besides! Let us say half or even more.

In the garden of men Saints was a gathering of Confessors of the Faith belonging to no hierarchy either religious, civil or military, and in the garden of women Saints was to be found the greater part of those Saints the Church defines negatively, calling them "neither virgins nor martyrs." This was the immense crowd of those good souls who, on Earth, had lived simply, and even with a certain mediocrity, and sometimes even naughtily or even wickedly by committing many mortal sins. For many it was the Communion of Saints which had saved them at the last moment. Though these were the least of the Saints in Heaven, they realized that for what they had done during their lives on Earth, it was they who were best rewarded.

Jamie, as if in a marvelous dream, crossed through these crowds greeted with the same affectionate welcome. He was pleasantly chided for his little lie, and so as if to scold him one would tease: "Oh, what a naughty little boy!" or another would prophesy: "This tiny fellow has a great future before him; he'll go a long way."

Agnes presented him to his ancestors, to several of his aunts in particular who went on raving about him. Jamie was really touched to hear praise like he used to hear on Earth—"How you resemble your grandfather!"—"You have the eyes of your grand aunt on your mother's side." or—"When this child laughs you'd swear it was his grandmother when she was his age!"

There is no end to discovering resemblances, especially in Paradise; everyone meets his ancestors—all the way back to Adam!

Jamie was astonished not to feel the least bit tired, he had been walking a long while and at each step found himself being hugged. Before, in family reunions, he had never been very fond of being embraced by a swarm of kinfolk whose faces did not always seem very friendly. He had even been scolded a few times for having pouted, and, all in all, would have preferred to have been sent outdoors to play. But here everybody was so kind; and as for himself he felt happy, alert and full of the desire to be polite to everyone.

The last two gardens in the back kept Jamie and Agnes a long while. The Blessed in these two gardens, after having smothered Jamie with a thousand hugs and kisses, took advantage of the occasion to ask Saint Agnes all kinds of questions. They spoke of all sorts of things that were too difficult for Jamie. So instead of listening, Jamie looked towards the Lord and Our Lady, he talked with them at a distance without saying a thing, or else repeating the same words with as much love as he was capable of. He said to Our Lady, "Hail Mother Mary..."

Now it happened that while he was turned towards the Lord and the Virgin Mary an endless procession of Saints filed before the throne of God. They were accompanying a very venerable Saint, a very glorious Saint, perhaps it was Abraham himself... yes, it was certainly he, with his long beard.

The Lord had called him near to Himself, and when the "Father of the faithful" was honored by the Lord there was always an abundance of joy and light cast upon all of the Saints of Paradise. Abraham knelt down before the Lord, and Jesus spoke tenderly with him a good while. At the same time an immense gladness spread throughout the gardens.

And behold, an extraordinary thing came to pass: all of the Saints in Paradise cried out together: "Glory be to the Father and to the Son and to the Holy Spirit."

This wonderful chant, which Jamie heard then for the first time, overwhelmed him. It was like a great light in his soul, a new revelation, a new vision of God and of all things, because suddenly the Holy Trinity appeared to him.

How did it appear?

Jamie did not know at first; but then the Lord, having glanced at him, unveiled the mystery of His holy Face whose look had so profoundly transformed and renewed him at his arrival in Paradise, filling him with the blessed life he now enjoyed. Jamie understood, then, that this was the face of the Trinity! This extraordinary operation, so powerful and so gentle, which the Lord's glance had accomplished in him, was the work of the Trinity. In the eyes of Jesus were to be found the Father, the Son and the Holy Ghost; and They were contemplating in Jamie a beloved creature, well conformed to the divine model.

Jamie had a better grasp, now. How annoying to be a child! You understand things so slowly, so very slowly... But maybe this progressive development of understanding and of love was normal for everyone. You just cannot know everything at once! He had already come to know so many things since he was there.

Anyway, Jamie certainly did not feel the slightest shadow of sadness or displeasure; he only saw the enormous gain he had made and the incredible increase in happiness which was the result.

Joyfully following the progress of her little brother, Agnes whispered to herself: "Oh, so glad I am! Look, he has started to open his eyes."

In fact, Jamie had seen and known the Trinity from the first instant; but now he saw It, understood It and loved It infinitely better—more consciously, more attentively, more fully. He could no longer take his eyes off the Lord Jesus, but remained forever contemplating this superabundant source of his whole being and happiness.

Despite the great distance from Jesus' throne, it seemed to Jamie as though he were right up close. It was like having two ways of seeing: for the eyes there was one distance—and he knew that it would take many little steps to find himself at Jesus' feet, whereas for the eyes of his soul, of his heart, there was no distance—and, it was like a permanent, direct, intimate and infinitely sweet contact with the Lord Jesus.

Jamie, led by the hand, followed Agnes from garden to garden, and never did the vision of the serene Trinity fade from his mind. The eyes of the Lord seemed to reveal to him more and more of the secrets of His divine beauty; This look so human and so divine, this single and threefold look, this look so simple and so profound, so joyful, tender, beautiful, pure, was laden with silent words that Jamie alone heard in his heart, as if he were the sole Saint in Paradise. It was like a sweet fascination lovingly captivating Jamie's eyes.

The Father, the Son and the Holy Ghost, together yet each distinctly, told Jamie all the love They had for him, and the joy They found in making him happy. They told him how, from all eternity, They had loved, desired—as one desires someone without whom one would be unhappy—prepared and organized all things in Heaven and on Earth so that he would not be lost, but on the contrary, quickly take his place in the midst of Them, and forever.

The Three seemed to open Their circle to let Jamie enter. They gave Themselves to him and by His sole glance the Lord Jesus came, and with His love filled Jamie's little heart to overflowing.

Then Jamie opened wide his heart so that his God could enter and make His dwelling there forever.

❀ ❀ ❀ ❀ ❀

When, after a very long moment—which seemed very long to him anyway—like after having drunk from a flowing spring, little Jamie looked around and found that his vision of Paradise had changed completely, to the point that he could no longer recognize it.

Now that the eyes of his soul were open he could no longer close them! It was as if a new world had revealed itself to him, a world whose richness and splendor surpassed everything that he had already seen.

What he first saw when he turned his eyes away from the Lord was an angel. In fact it was his own Guardian Angel. It was a moment of surprise...

"Well," said Agnes, "aren't you going to say anything to your own Guardian Angel?"

Long ago Jamie had learned three prayers: the Our Father, the Hail Mary and an invocation to his Holy Guardian Angel; but he well understood that it was not like that that one spoke to an Angel. In a wink Jamie showed the Angel how much he loved him and how glad he was to see him. He did this in the proper way, because with Angels you speak not with words, but soul to spirit.

Almost at the same time, Jamie saw (not with his eyes, but with his soul) myriads of Angels, Angels everywhere: in the air, on the ground, in the sea; and around the Lord was an immense, living halo of Angels; and the living light which had so dazzled Jamie earlier on, was resplendent with Angels of an incomparable brilliance.

In this way a new category of the Blessed inhabitants of Paradise revealed itself to Jamie, seeking his love and surrounding him with theirs. All of these Angels loved Jaime very much, because there is a certain similarity between Angels and little children. To think that from the beginning he had been surrounded by and plunged into so much love, and that only now was he starting to notice! Truly, the more he knew, the more there remained to learn!

Jamie laughed; he would have liked to say hello to each Angel. Nothing was easier than to make their acquaintance. No need to walk among them as with the Saints, a simple movement of the heart and you entered immediately into contact with each one of them.

This discovery of the Angels completed in a special way his vision of Paradise; but this vision was also changed by the revelation of the shining souls of the Blessed. All of these souls became visible to Jamie in the same manner as the Angels had become visible. He could speak with each one in a way that, up until then, had only been possible with the Lord and Our Lady. A simple look, replacing all words by silence, permitted his soul to be in touch with other souls, and his inner eye to perceive the spiritual beauty which shone out from their glorious souls. He learned new songs of praise and adoration, and he felt himself being swept away in a current of light and life.

The secret beauty of all these things was now completely unveiled. Everywhere Jamie discovered the beloved sign, the image, the seal, the splendid reflection of the Holy Trinity. The unity of the creation and the glory due to the Creator could be read everywhere. Even in inanimate things Jamie saw the joy of their belonging to God. Fountains praised Him; flowing waters spoke blessings to Him; precious stones wanted to be pretty for Him alone; and flowers, bowing their petals, offered sweets smells to Him. All was God's; it gave itself to God; creatures everywhere were nestled and pressed about the Trinity, in the shadow of this infinite tenderness. In these gardens, surrounded by hill-tops forming a kind of cloister, one felt at home, at home with God, buried, hidden in His light, in His living joy.

Outside of Paradise what could there be to see? Certainly nothing very interesting, nothing beautiful, nothing joyful: all being was concentrated here, and it seemed to Jamie that he had become all eyes to see with, and all heart to love with.

❈ ❈ ❈ ❈ ❈

Meanwhile, Agnes and Jamie were continuing their walk from garden to garden, when, right in front of them, there rose a great heap of gold cups and vessels of incense all ready for the next liturgy. Again Jamie's curiosity, forgetting the general view, was captivated by all of these preparations.

"Look," said Agnes, "this is the garden that offers incense of adoration before the Holy Trinity. You'll see, it's very beautiful!"

And truly it was going to be beautiful. Jamie posed a question:

—"But when is it the children's turn to offer incense?"

—"Well, never! You never offer incense because you are too little, but there are always many children carrying lamps, so sooner or later it will be your turn."

—"And what do you do with the lamps?"

—"For once you do whatever you like—which doesn't add very much to the ceremony, but that's just my opinion. I've tried so often to organize what you children are to do, but it's impossible with children. Half of you leave your lamps just anywhere and go climbing the steps of the throne to nap here and there at Our Lady's feet. Finally, I think she likes things better that way, because nearly every time she takes one of you in Her arms and rocks him to sleep—lucky little fellow, that one!"

—"And what do you do when you sleep?"

—"What do you do? Well, you sleep! But yes, I see what you mean... Listen; one day you will know what it is like, when this sleep overcomes you. In any case, I have often noticed that the children who have slept at the feet of Our Lady afterwards say things that astonish even me..." and, she added: "...even though I am beginning to understand little children, what with all the time that I have spent taking care of you!"

Little Jamie was no longer listening. His eyes were fixed upon those of his tender Mother Mary, and without saying anything he was asking in his heart for the favor of sleeping this mysterious sleep near her, about which Agnes knew nothing, because it was the privilege of little children. From afar Our Lady assured him: "All right, all right"; and Her smile was full of a special kindness.

The tour of Paradise was coming to a close. Jamie had been hugged and kissed an incalculable number of times, but in Heaven you never get tired of anything and the enjoyment found at first continues to be pure and intense to the last. Besides, in

Heaven you do not suffer from repetition; everything is always new, and nothing begins over again with monotony, as on Earth. Time itself is unperceived, because you always remain in an unchangeable present: a thousand years are as one day, and for the Blessed, a thousand kisses are like one kiss, and one kiss like a thousand.

Agnes had accomplished her mission and could give Jamie back to Tarcisius; but before parting, she leaned down gently over her little brother and said, "Do you love me too?"

"Oh, yes!" said Jamie; and he embraced her with all his heart.

"There you go," said Agnes, "Now I'm going to leave you with Tarcisius, all right? But you know, in Paradise we always remain together anyway; when we leave each other, we do not separate."

Then they went towards the group of children where Tarcisius was playing.

Agnes continued: "Here, Tarcisius; I'm entrusting Jamie to you. He is very nice, and will be happy to play with you." And she added: "As for me, I must run and see what is going on around the fountain; three or four children have surely fallen in."

And at once she was off, on light and rapid feet, looking important as young girls do when they play at being mothers with their little brothers.

~ ~ ~ ~ ~

"Come on, Jamie," said Tarcisius taking him by the hand, "you see, we are playing 'palms'. Do you know how to play?"

—"No."

—"We'll show you how, then; it's not hard. Just stand here and hold on to your palm branch. All you have to do is watch the others and imitate them."

While explaining, he placed Jamie in a long line of small boys and gave him a handsome green palm branch which he was to hold straight up, in front of him.

"Attention now," said Tarcisius; "everybody ready?"

—"Tarcisius! Tarcisius!"

—"What now?"

—"I broke my palm!"

A small boy with curly blond hair was yelling like this. In his chubby little hands were the two pitiful halves of his green palm branch. It was astonishing that such a little boy could have succeeded in breaking so large a palm—it was three times bigger than he was. It was probably a bit broken before.

Jamie was getting used to the way people acted in Paradise, and it was not at all surprised to see the little boy unashamed and obliged to make no excuses. He was not even scolded for having broken his toy. On the contrary, everyone laughed when they saw the two halves of the palm branch, and the little boy laughed more than anyone else.

Tarcisius spoke up: "Listen everybody; you are all going to stay put in your places while we go mend this palm. When we get back, we'll begin the game all over." And to the boy at fault: "You, come with me."

Tarcisius lead the curly haired boy who, laughing all the while, carried the two halves of his palm branch as they went up towards the throne.

They addressed themselves to Our Lady, which is the universal rule, as one should always begin by her. Our Lady handed the palm to the Lord, who laughed and glued it together by simply joining the two ends. Next the Blessed Virgin picked up the little boy, hugged him and presented him to the Lord for a blessing. Our Lord kept him a while on his knees.

In the mean time, Tarcisius, being a big boy, stood near his Mother; she had slipped an arm around his shoulder as they spoke together. The small children who had stayed in the garden watched all this and were very happy. Finally, Tarcisius got down on his knees in front of the Lord as He traced the sign of the cross on his forehead. Afterwards, accompanied by the little curly haired boy, he returned to the Children's Garden; and behold! The little boy's branch had become the most beautiful of them all, and filled the children present with amazement.

Finally the game began. Jamie was really interested and ready to do his best, looking to see how the others played. Before long Tarcisius stopped and said to him, "Oh, my poor little Jamie, that's not the way we play. You should always watch the Lord."

Jamie stopped.

How were they to play and watch the Lord at the same time? Since he had been in Paradise he, like everyone else, was submitted to this law: the Lord was always present to his vision, and that from the first instant in which the light of Heaven had struck his eyes. But he had no continual consciousness of this vision; or rather, there was not yet a conscious fusion of all his thoughts and acts with the action of this perpetual vision. Now it was as though a veil had been lifted from his eyes.

Jamie understood then that his first initiation was completed: from now on he would experience life to its fullest, there was no longer in him even the slightest separation between himself as creature and God, his Creator. And this perfect union englobed, so to speak, everything in Paradise: in God Jamie saw, possessed and enjoyed all things.

Once again he saw all of these grand gardens surrounding the throne; he saw them in God; and what he saw was beyond words—as if on all things had risen the pure light of an eternal springtime.

In one glimpse he beheld all the Saints and Angels who, seeing him, begged him not to delay in joining them in their song of praise to the dearly beloved Lord. Jamie had grown to become a big boy—yes he had; he knew everything now, and was going to take part, like everyone else, in the concert of eternity.

Jamie was overwhelmed with joy when he thought about the new way he now had to tell the Lord Jesus and the most Holy Trinity how much love he had for them in his heart. All of the heavenly court saw this and rejoiced. Jamie understood that these things were bound up in the substantial unity of the Father, the Son and the Holy Spirit.

Truly God was all in all, and in no way could one isolate himself from this unique and blessed company.

Yes, Jamie knew everything now.

"Come on," said Tarcisius, "let's play, and don't go thinking that little boys like you know everything! You'll see: eternity never ends! Nor do the revelations which God has reserved for you. You cannot imagine how happy one can be..."

Saint Tarcisius had begun his work: teaching his little brother.

So little Jamie,
taking his palm to play,
his eyes dazzled by the radiant light,
his heart bursting with boundless joy,
opened his little mouth,
joined the myriad of myriads of blessed Saints,
and began to sing the eternal ALLELUIA!

www.ingramcontent.com/pod-product-compliance
Lightning Source LLC
Chambersburg PA
CBHW030518100426
42813CB00001B/77